ROLL

OF

EMPLOYEES WHO SERVED

IN

His Majesty's

NAVAL, MILITARY AND AIR FORCES

1914—1918.

ARTHUR GUINNESS, SON & CO., LIMITED,

DUBLIN.

INTRODUCTION.

THE purpose of this little volume is to preserve, in a suitable form, a record of those in the employment of Messrs. Arthur Guinness, Son & Company, Limited, who gave their services—and in many instances, their lives—for the defence of the Empire at the most perilous and critical period of its history.

It is also intended as a token of gratitude and honour. Inadequate though it may be in this respect, it is proffered, and will no doubt be accepted, as a modest tribute on the part of the Company to the courage and sacrifice of those whose loyalty and devotion it commemorates. To measure the debt due, whether individually or collectively, to those named herein is impossible, but to acknowledge it is an elementary duty.

No grade of the Company's service is absent from the Roll. Each has its representatives. The distribution of the

names according to department, for convenience of reference, is the sole attempt at classification, for it was felt that any other differentiation would be invidious where all were united in a single aim.

Pains have not been spared to ensure the accuracy of the record, and it is hoped that the Roll is not marred by any omission or oversight.

The Great War of 1914—1918 commenced, so far as the United Kingdom is concerned, on the 4th August, 1914. It continued for four years, three months and seven days, until the 11th November, 1918, when, the Central European Powers having appealed for an armistice, the last shot was fired. The victory of the Allied and Associated Powers was complete, and peace was signed at Versailles on the 28th June, 1919.

Of the causes of the War, its vicissitudes and results, its glories and its griefs, this is not the place to speak. For the magnitude of its operations by sea, land and air, for the far-reaching gravity of its consequences (as yet but dimly appre-

hended) recorded history furnishes no parallel, and to distant generations must be left the task of appraising the effects of the struggle, not only upon individuals, families and nations, but upon the human race itself.

More than eight hundred servants of the Company took their places in the Imperial Forces. Scattered over the world, afloat and ashore, with lofty tasks or lowly, all rendered honourable service, and more than one hundred laid down their lives.

To those who fell we render reverent homage; to those who survive we offer this small, but none the less sincere, expression of heartfelt gratitude.

JAMES'S GATE, DUBLIN.

December, 1920.

BOARD OF DIRECTORS.

NAME.	RANK.	REGIMENT.	DECORATION.
Elveden, The Viscount, C.B., C.M.G., M.P.	Captain ...	... Royal Naval Volunteer Reserve	A.D.C. to H.M. the King, 1916—1918
Guinness, The Honble., W. E., M.P.	Lieut.-Colonel	... The Duke of York's Own Loyal Suffolk Hussars	Distinguished Service Order and Bar. Mentioned in Despatches three times.

ACCOUNTANT'S DEPARTMENT.

NAME.	RANK.	REGIMENT.	DECORATION.
Atkinson, C. B.	Sub-Lieutenant ...	Royal Naval Volunteer Reserve (Auxiliary Patrol)	—
***Birmingham, W. A.** ...	2nd Lieutenant ...	6th Royal Irish Fusiliers ...	—
Bright, H. S.	Captain	Machine Gun Corps	Military Cross. Mentioned in Despatches twice.
Hill, C. L.	Lieutenant	Royal Field Artillery	—
Middleton, A. H. ...	Lieutenant	Royal Munster Fusiliers ...	—
Troy, D. F.	Sergeant	Royal Army Medical Corps ...	—
***Ward, B. L.**	Corporal	2nd Royal Dublin Fusiliers ...	—

AUDIT DEPARTMENT.

NAME.	RANK.	REGIMENT.	DECORATION.
Burkitt, R. F.	Major	Royal Garrison Artillery (S.R.)	Military Cross.
Clarke, P. B. C.	2nd Lieutenant ...	11th Royal Dublin Fusiliers ...	—
Fisher, C. G. C.	Captain	Royal Dublin Fusiliers... ...	Military Cross.
Holland E. F. J.	Lieutenant	9th Royal Irish Rifles	Military Cross.
Kelly, G. W.	Captain	Royal Army Service Corps ...	—
Macnie, W. R.	Lieutenant	5th Royal Irish Fusiliers ...	—
Moorhead, J. F. ...	Captain	Royal Army Service Corps ..	—
Wood, N.	Sergeant	7th Royal Dublin Fusiliers ...	—

BREWHOUSE DEPARTMENT.

NAME.	RANK.	REGIMENT.	DECORATION.
Armstrong, Edward ...	Lance-Corporal ...	1st Irish Guards	—
Bannister, E.C.	Lieutenant	Royal Army Service Corps ...	—
***Bligh, Thomas**	Guardsman... ...	2nd Battalion Coldstream Guards	—
***Boland, John**	Sergeant	2nd Irish Guards	—
Bowyer, P. G.	2nd Lieutenant ...	5th City of London (London Rifle Brigade)	—
Brien, Michael	Staff-Sergeant ...	Royal Army Medical Corps ...	—
Brien, William	Gunner	Royal Field Artillery	—

*** Killed in action or died of wounds.**

BREWHOUSE DEPARTMENT *(continued)*.

NAME.	RANK.	REGIMENT.	DECORATION.
Browne, Andrew, J. W.	Private	Royal Air Force...	—
Browner, Thomas ...	Attendant	Royal Naval Sick Berth Reserve	—
Buckley, Francis ...	Petty Officer, 1st class	Royal Naval Sick Berth Reserve	—
***Burke, John**	Trooper	2nd Dragoon Guards	—
Burns, Martin	Able-bodied Seaman	Royal Naval Sick Berth Reserve	—
Buttanshaw, C.	Lieutenant	Royal Garrison Artillery ...	—
***Byrne, Laurence** ...	Private	Royal Army Medical Corps ...	—
Byrne, Patrick	Sergeant	Royal Army Medical Corps ...	Mentioned in Despatches.
Callan, William	Sergeant	Military Police, Staff Corps ...	—
Chant, Harry	Private	Royal Air Force...	—
Coghlan, James... ...	Private	Royal Army Service Corps ...	—
Collins, Edward... ...	Trooper	4th Hussars	—
Comerford, Patrick ...	Driver	Royal Army Service Corps (M.T.)	—
Conway, Charles ...	Corporal	Royal Field Artillery	—
***Conville, Patrick** ...	Gunner	Royal Garrison Artillery ...	—
Coote, C. R. P.	Major	Royal Army Service Corps ... (36th Ulster Division)	Mentioned in Despatches, May 1917 Belgian Croix de Guerre, Feb. 1919
Coyne, Francis	Corporal	1st Irish Guards...	Military Medal.
Cullen, Thomas	Private	Royal Army Medical Corps ...	—
Curran, John	Sergeant	2nd Royal Irish Regiment ...	—
Curran, Christopher ...	Attendant	Royal Naval Sick Berth Reserve	—
Dalton, E. C.	Lance-Corporal ...	3rd Royal Irish Rifles	—
Daly, Daniel	Private	3rd Royal Dublin Fusiliers ...	—
Darlington, William ...	Quarter-Master Sgt.	Royal Army Medical Corps ...	Mentioned in Despatches
Delaney, Richard ...	Gunner	Royal Garrison Artillery ...	—
Donnelly, Joseph ...	Sergeant	7th Royal Irish Rifles	—
Doyle, Joseph	Corporal	1st Irish Guards...	—
Dunne, Michael... ...	Garrison Sgt.-Major	Royal Dublin Fusiliers... ...	—
Edwards, Richard ...	Private	Royal Air Force...	—
Farrell, Joseph... ...	Corporal	6th Royal Dublin Fusiliers ...	—
Franks, A. G.	Staff-Sergeant ...	Royal Army Service Corps ...	—
***Geoghegan, William** ...	Sergeant	Royal Dublin Fusiliers	—
Geraghty, Thomas ...	Pioneer	Royal Engineers...	—
Gray, P. W.	Sergeant	9th Royal Irish Fusiliers ...	Military Medal.

*** Killed in action or died of wounds.**

BREWHOUSE DEPARTMENT *(continued).*

NAME.	RANK.	REGIMENT.	DECORATION.
Gully, John	Petty Officer, 1st class	Royal Naval Sick Berth Reserve	—
Harrington, Patrick ...	Quarter-Master Sgt.	Royal Army Medical Corps ...	—
Heycock, M. S.	Captain	9th Battalion Rifle Brigade ...	Military Cross.
Hildebrand, W. H. ...	Lieutenant	11th Royal Welsh Fusiliers ...	—
Hogan, Michael	Corporal	2nd Royal Dublin Fusiliers ...	—
Howlett, Alfred	Company Sgt.-Major	2nd Essex Regiment	—
Hughes, Anthony ...	Gunner	Royal Field Artillery	—
Hynes, Patrick	Private	2nd Leinster Regiment	—
Ireland, William ...	Corporal	Royal Garrison Artillery ...	—
***Johnston, Robert** ...	Trooper	5th Lancers	—
***Kavanagh, James** ...	Guardsman	1st Irish Guards	—
Keeley, James	Sergeant	Connaught Rangers	—
Kelly, William	Sergeant	10th Royal Dublin Fusiliers ...	—
Kidd, E. L.	Lieutenant	Royal Field Artillery	—
Kilfoyle, William ...	Corporal	8th Hussars	—
King, Timothy	Private	Royal Army Medical Corps ...	—
Kinnear, William ...	Gunner	Royal Garrison Artillery ...	Mentioned in Despatches.
Larminie, J. P. A. ...	Lieutenant	Royal Field Artillery	—
***Leslie, Robert**	Sergeant	11th Inniskilling Fusiliers ...	—
Lott, Thomas	Sergeant	2nd Irish Guards	—
***Mahon, Matthew** ...	Guardsman	2nd Irish Guards	—
Mahon, Richard ...	Sergeant	South Irish Horse	—
Mann, J. G.	Captain	Royal Army Service Corps ...	Mentioned in Despatches twice.
Martin, Peter	Sergeant	Worcester Regiment	—
Murphy, John	Private	3rd Leinster Regiment	Mentioned in *London Gazette*, "For valuable services rendered in the War."
Murray, John	Battery Sgt.-Major..	Royal Field Artillery	—
McAree, P. J.	Corporal	Irish Guards	—
McDonnell, John ...	Gunner	Royal Field Artillery	—
McManus, Thomas ...	Quarter-Master Sgt.	Royal Engineers	—
McSherry, Michael ...	Lance-Corporal ...	2nd Irish Guards	—
Newbold, C. J.	Lieutenant-Colonel	Royal Engineers	D.S.O. Mentioned in Despatches three times.

* **Killed in action or died of wounds.**

BREWHOUSE DEPARTMENT *(continued)*.

Name.	Rank.	Regiment.	Decoration.
***Noble, John** ...	Guardsman...	1st Irish Guards...	—
O'Connor, John...	Guardsman...	2nd Irish Guards	—
Paul, H.	Lieutenant ...	5th Duke of Wellington's (W.R.) Regiment (attached Special Brigade Royal Engineers)	—
Peake, E. G. ...	Major ...	Royal Engineers...	O.B.E. Mentioned in Despatches twice.
Redmond, Stephen	Gunner ...	Royal Horse Artillery	—
***Reddy, Francis** ...	Corporal ...	1st Yorks. and Lancs. Regiment	—
Robinet, Charles	Corporal ...	3rd Royal Dublin Fusiliers ...	—
Roche, Cecil ...	2nd Lieutenant	Royal Dublin Fusiliers... ...	—
Ryan, Andrew ...	Guardsman...	1st Irish Guards...	—
***Ryan, William** ...	Guardsman...	1st Irish Guards...	—
Scally, Edward ...	Sergeant ...	Leinster Regiment	—
Seddall, R. F. ...	Captain ...	Royal Army Service Corps (24th Divisional Train)	Mentioned in Despatches.
***Shiel, C.**	Lieutenant ...	Royal Air Force...	—
Shildrick, L. R. ...	Major ...	2nd Royal Munsters	Mentioned in Despatches.
Shirley, Henry ...	Sergeant ...	Royal Army Medical Corps ...	—
***Sinclair, Alexander**	Sergeant ...	6th Connaught Rangers ...	—
Smyth, John ...	Guardsman...	1st Irish Guards...	—
Somerfield, E. ...	Captain ...	16th Royal Irish Rifles... ...	—
***Stafford, Francis**	Rifleman ...	6th Royal Irish Rifles	—
Stafford, George	Private ...	10th Royal Dublin Fusiliers ...	—
Stephens, Robert H.	Petty Officer, 1st class	Royal Naval Sick Berth Reserve	—
Switzer, Robert	Captain ...	7th Royal Irish Regiment ...	Military Cross. Meritorious Service Medal.
Tait, William ...	2nd Lieutenant	Tank Corps	—
Tanham, Bernard	Private ...	6th Leinster Regiment	—
Thornton, J. J. ...	Chief Petty Officer...	Royal Naval Auxiliary Sick Berth Reserve	—
Toner, James ...	Sergeant ...	Royal Field Artillery	—
Turnbull, James A.	Private ...	Royal Army Medical Corps ...	—
Waugh, C. S. ...	Lieutenant ...	The King's Own Yorkshire Light Infantry	—
Weeks, O. H. ...	Captain ...	Royal Air Force	—
Wilson, George ...	Private ...	10th Royal Dublin Fusiliers ...	—
Woods, George F.	Guardsman...	2nd Irish Guards	Distinguished Service Medal.

*** Killed in action or died of wounds.**

CASH OFFICE.

NAME.	RANK.	REGIMENT.	DECORATION.
Johnson, R. S.	Lieutenant	1st London Regt. (Roy. Fusiliers)	—
Jolley, W. E.	Sub-Lieutenant ...	Royal Naval Volunteer Reserve	—

CASK DEPARTMENT.

NAME.	RANK.	REGIMENT.	DECORATION.
Allan, D.	Private	Royal Army Medical Corps ...	—
Dykes, R.	Lieutenant	6th Black Watch (Royal Highlanders)	—
Giffin, W. C. D.	Lieutenant	2nd Royal Irish Regiment ...	**Distinguished Service Order. Military Cross. Mentioned in Despatches.**
***Howard, George** ...	Private	10th Royal Dublin Fusiliers ...	—
Kerrigan, W. J. ...	Corporal	Royal Army Medical Corps ...	—
Mooney, R. T.	Acting-Corporal ...	1st Royal Dublin Fusiliers ...	—
McAree, J.	Pioneer	Royal Engineers...	—
Rawson, R.	Lance-Corporal ...	10th Royal Dublin Fusiliers ...	—
Tyrrell, P. J.	Staff Sergeant ...	Royal Army Medical Corps ...	—
Walker, Henry	Corporal	Royal Army Medical Corps ...	—
Wallace, J. J.	Lieutenant	Royal Army Service Corps ...	—
***Yarnell, V. F. H.** ...	Trooper	South Irish Horse	—

COOKE'S LANE MALTINGS.

NAME.	RANK.	REGIMENT.	DECORATION.
Byrne, John	Lance-Corporal ...	2nd Royal Welsh Fusiliers ...	—
Doonan, William ...	Guardsman... ...	1st Irish Guards...	—
Hennessy, Thomas ...	Sergeant	6th Dragoon Guards	—
***Holt, John H.**	Private	2/6th North Stafford Regiment	—
***Kennedy, James** ...	Private	1st Royal Dublin Fusiliers ...	—
Nolan, John	Guardsman... ...	2nd Irish Guards	—
Powderly, Christopher W.	Sergeant	4th King's Own Liverpool Regt.	—

*** Killed in action or died of wounds.**

CHANNEL STEAMER SERVICE.

NAME.	RANK.	REGIMENT.	DECORATION.
***Davey, Fredk. W.** ...	Able Seaman ...	Royal Naval Reserve	—
Kelly, John	Able Seaman ...	H.M.S. "Bacchus"	Mentioned in Despatches.
***Kendall, Ernest A.** ...	Able Seaman ...	Royal Naval Reserve	—
McIlwaine, James ...	Lance-Corporal ...	15th Royal Irish Rifles	—

COOPERAGE DEPARTMENT.

NAME.	RANK.	REGIMENT.	DECORATION.
Allen, George	Sergeant	Royal Army Medical Corps ...	—
Anderson, James ...	Private	Royal Army Medical Corps ...	—
Ball, John	Private	9th Duke of Cornwall's Light Infantry	—
Brady, William	Gunner	153rd Batt. Royal Garr. Artillery	—
***Brien, Patrick**	Sergeant	6th Royal Dublin Fusiliers ...	—
Byrne, Bernard... ...	Private	54th Field Ambulance (R.A.M.C.)	—
Byrne, Denis	Trooper	1st Dragoon Guards	—
Byrne, Henry	Sergeant	8th Hussars	—
Byrne, Myles	Private	8th Royal Dublin Fusiliers ...	—
Byrne, William	Private	Royal Army Medical Corps ...	—
Brown, Edward ...	Gunner	Royal Field Artillery	—
Brown, Samuel	Sergeant	56th Brigade Royal Field Artilly.	—
Campbell, James ...	Private	5th Royal Dublin Fusiliers ...	—
***Carlson, Wilson V.** ...	Private	Tank Corps	—
Carr, Joseph	Private	2nd Royal Dublin Fusiliers ...	—
Carroll, Maurice ...	Trooper	Scots Greys	—
Carroll, Michael ...	S. Q. M. Sergeant...	Royal Engineers...	—
Carroll, Michael J. ...	Corporal	Royal Engineers...	—
Clarke, Christopher ...	Lance-Corporal ...	2nd Royal Irish Regiment ...	—
Cleary, Thomas... ...	Lance-Corporal ...	1st Royal Irish Regiment ...	—
Coffey, James	Able-bodied Seaman	Royal Navy	—
Connolly, Thomas ...	Sergeant	2nd Royal Dublin Fusiliers ...	—
Connolly, Thomas ...	Private	Royal Army Medical Corps ...	—
Cosgrove, James ...	Sapper	Royal Engineers...	—
Culverhouse, Francis ...	Corporal	Royal Army Medical Corps ...	—
Cunningham, Henry ...	Trooper	6th Inniskilling Dragoons ...	—
Cunningham, Thomas ...	Guardsman... ...	1st Irish Guards...	—
Curran, Nicholas ...	Gunner	Royal Horse Artillery	—

* **Killed in action or died of wounds.**

COOPERAGE DEPARTMENT *(continued)*.

NAME.	RANK.	REGIMENT.	DECORATION.
Daly, Thomas	Trooper	1st Life Guards	—
Delaney, Edward ...	Sapper	Royal Engineers...	—
Delaney, Joseph ...	Lance-Corporal ...	2nd Royal Irish Rifles	—
Doyle, John	Private	6th East Lancs.	—
Doyle, Patrick	Trooper	4th Hussars	—
Dunne, Patrick	Sapper	Royal Engineers...	—
Dunne, Stephen	Private	Royal Army Service Corps (M.T.)	—
Dunphy, Patrick ...	Gunner	Royal Garrison Artillery ...	—
Farrelly, Patrick ...	Sergeant	3rd Royal Irish Fusiliers ...	—
***Foran, Thomas J.** ...	Private	Royal Army Medical Corps ...	—
***Foster, John**	Rifleman	1st Royal Irish Rifles	—
Fox, Patrick	Guardsman... ...	2nd Irish Guards	—
Gogarty, Francis ...	Acting-Corporal ...	Royal Army Medical Corps ...	—
Halford, Francis ...	Corporal	Royal Army Medical Corps ...	—
Hanlon, Peter	Sergeant	8th Royal Irish Fusiliers ...	—
***Heffernan, Martin** ...	Private	9th Royal Dublin Fusiliers ...	—
Hegarty, Joseph ...	Private	Royal Army Medical Corps ...	—
Helly, John	Steward	Naval Sick Berth	—
Hendrick, Patrick J. ...	Gunner	Royal Garrison Artillery ...	—
Hill, Joseph	Corporal	Royal Engineers...	Distinguished Conduct Medal. Military Medal.
***Hoare, Joseph**	Guardsman... ...	1st Irish Guards	—
Hogan, Joseph	Private	Royal Army Medical Corps ...	—
Hogan, Michael	Private	2nd Batt. Royal Dublin Fusiliers	—
***Hopkins, James**... ...	Private	8th Royal Dublin Fusiliers ...	—
Joyce, Augustine ...	Sapper	Royal Engineers...	—
Kavanagh, Thomas ...	Trooper	4th Hussars	—
Keeble, Albert	Sergeant	1st Wiltshire Regiment... ...	—
Kelly, Michael	Private	21st Royal Scots Fusiliers ...	—
Kelly, Michael	Corporal	Royal Irish Regiment	—
***Kerr, William**	Private	Royal Army Medical Corps ...	—
King, Charles	Corporal	26th Batty. Royal Field Artillery	—
Lacey, Edward	Guardsman... ...	1st Irish Guards	—

*** Killed in action or died of wounds.**

COOPERAGE DEPARTMENT *(continued)*.

NAME.	RANK.	REGIMENT.	DECORATION.
*Leahy, John ...	... Guardsman...	... 1st Irish Guards	—
Lynch, Thomas ...	... Sapper ...	... Royal Engineers...	Military Medal.
Moore, Thomas ...	... Private ...	... Royal Army Medical Corps ...	—
Morgan, Joseph...	... Lance-Corporal	... 34th Machine Gun Battery ...	—
*Mulligan, Alexander	... Private ...	... 2nd Royal Inniskilling Fusiliers	—
Mullins, Fergus ...	... Private ...	... 8th Royal Dublin Fusiliers ...	—
*Murphy, Thomas	... Driver ...	... Royal Field Artillery	—
Murray, Robert...	... Corporal ...	... Royal Army Medical Corps ...	—
McDonald, William	... Private ...	... 2nd Connaught Rangers ...	—
McEnnally, James	... Corporal ...	... 2nd Royal Munster Fusiliers ...	—
McFarlane, William	... Sapper ...	... Royal Engineers...	—
McGuire, John ...	... Guardsman ...	... 1st Irish Guards	—
*McIvor, James ...	... Rifleman ...	... 12th King's Royal Rifles ...	—
*Nelson, William R.	... Sapper ...	... Royal Engineers...	—
*Niland, Joseph ...	... Sapper ...	... Royal Engineers...	—
Nolan, Arthur ...	... Sergeant ...	... 1st Royal Dublin Fusiliers ...	—
O'Connor, James	... Private ...	... 5th Battn. Royal Irish Regiment	—
O'Connor, John P.	... Private ...	... Royal Army Medical Corps ...	—
O'Dea, Michael ...	... Private ...	... Royal Army Service Corps ...	—
*O'Rourke, Peter	... Corporal ...	... 2nd Irish Guards	—
*O'Toole, James ...	... Private ...	... 8th Royal Dublin Fusiliers ...	—
Ormonde, Philip	... Gunner ...	... 112th Heavy Battery Royal Field Artillery	—
Pinkerton, David	... Sapper ...	... Royal Engineers...	—
Powell, James ...	... Private ...	... 8th Royal Dublin Fusiliers ...	—
Powell, Joseph ...	... Private ...	... 43rd Royal Dublin Fusiliers ...	—
Price, Patrick ...	... Corporal ...	... Royal Army Medical Corps ...	—
Quinn, Bernard J.	... Sapper ...	... Royal Engineers...	—
Redmond, William	... Guardsman...	... 2nd Irish Guards	—
Russell, Dominick	... Private ...	... Labour Corps	—
*Ryan, Patrick ...	... Guardsman...	... 2nd Irish Guards	—
*Sheehan, William	... Rifleman ...	... 1st Battalion Rifle Brigade ...	—
Simpson, Michael	... Lance-Sergeant	... 2nd Irish Guards	—

*** Killed in action or died of wounds.**

COOPERAGE DEPARTMENT *(continued).*

Name.	Rank.	Regiment.	Decoration.
Smyth, Philip ...	... Gunner ...	... Royal Garrison Artillery ...	—
Stokes, John ...	... Gunner ...	... Royal Field Artillery ...	Croix de Guerre.
Stynes, Joseph ...	... Sergeant ...	... Royal Garrison Artillery ...	—
Tait, Thomas ..	... Company Sgt.-Major	8th Royal Dublin Fusiliers ...	Distinguished Conduct Medal. Military Medal.
Traynor, George	... Corporal ...	... Royal Army Medical Corps ...	—
Trimble, R. S. ...	... Lieutenant ...	... 6th Royal Irish Fusiliers ...	—
***Waters, Alexander**	... Sapper ...	... Royal Engineers...	—
***Whelan, Patrick**	... Private ...	... 2nd Royal Dublin Fusiliers ...	—
***White, John** ...	... Private ...	... 2nd Royal Irish Regiment ...	—
Woodhead, Charles	.. Sergeant ...	... 1st Irish Guards	—

ENGINEERS' DEPARTMENT.

Name.	Rank.	Regiment.	Decoration.
Amor, A. H. ...	... Lieutenant ...	... Royal Engineers...	—
Bluett, Sidney ...	... Sergeant ...	... Royal Army Medical Corps ...	—
***Boland, Patrick...**	... Rifleman ...	... 1st Royal Irish Rifles	—
Bray, Digby T. ...	... Sgt. Armourer, Staff	Royal Army Ordnance Corps ...	—
Breen, James ...	... Private ...	... Royal Army Medical Corps ...	—
Broderick, James	... Stoker ...	... Royal Navy	—
Byrne, James ...	... Private ...	... Royal West Kents	—
Byrne, Patrick J.	... Attendant ...	... Royal Naval Sick Berth Reserve	—
Bonny, John ...	... Corporal ...	... Royal Army Medical Corps ...	—
Burke, William ...	... Sergeant ...	... Leinsters	—
Carroll, William	... Corporal ...	... 7th Leinsters	Distinguished Conduct Medal. Military Medal.
Cashell, Robert ...	... Private ...	... Royal Army Medical Corps ...	—
Cawthra, H. ...	... Captain ...	... Royal Engineers...	Military Cross.
Christian, Patrick	... Gunner ...	... Royal Garrison Artillery ...	—
Coleman, Patrick	... Rifleman ...	... 2nd Royal Irish Rifles	—
Coole, William J.	... Corporal ...	... Royal Engineers...	—
Cooney, Thomas W.	... Lance-Corporal ...	Bedford's 13th Battalion ...	—
Corrin, Henry ...	... Guardsman ...	... Irish Guards	Distinguished Service Medal.
Costello, Martin	... Corporal ...	... Royal Garrison Artillery ...	—
Costello, Joseph	... Sergeant ...	... Royal Field Artillery	—

* **Killed in action or died of wounds.**

ENGINEERS' DEPARTMENT *(continued)*.

NAME.	RANK.	REGIMENT.	DECORATION.
Cronin, John	Steward	Royal Naval Sick Berth Reserve	—
Cullen, Frederick ...	Lance-Corporal ...	West Surrey	—
Dalgetty, A.	Sergeant	Royal Engineers...	—
Daly, Daniel J.	Sapper	Royal Engineers...	—
Daly, James	Private	East Kents	—
Delaney, Thomas ...	Rifleman	1st Royal Irish Rifles	—
Dennison, Patrick ...	Sergeant	10th North Staffs	—
Devitt, John	Senior Reserve Attendant.	Royal Naval Sick Berth Reserve	—
***Devoy, Michael**	Sergeant	9th King's Royal Rifle Corps ...	—
Dick, G.	Quarter-Master Sgt.	Royal Army Medical Corps ...	—
Doherty, Patrick ...	Private	Royal Army Medical Corps ...	—
Domican, John	Corporal	2nd Life Guards...	Military Medal.
***Domican, Richard** ...	Private	Royal Army Medical Corps ...	—
Doran, James	Trooper	1st Life Guards	—
Downes, James	Lance-Corporal ...	Royal Irish Fusiliers	—
Doyle, Christopher ...	Lance-Corporal ...	Royal Army Medical Corps ...	—
Doyle, John	Private	Royal Army Service Corps ...	—
***Doyle, Michael C.** ...	Attendant	Royal Naval Sick Berth Reserve	—
Doyle, Richard	Private	1st Connaught Rangers ...	—
Duffy, James	Sick Berth Attendant	Royal Naval Sick Berth Reserve	—
Duffy, Luke	Private	1st Royal Munster Fusiliers ...	—
Duke, John	Guardsman... ...	1st Irish Guards	—
Dunne, Peter	Sergeant	2nd Battalion Suffolk	—
Dunne, Thomas E. ...	Corporal	Royal Field Artillery	—
Durkin, Thomas ...	Corporal	Royal Irish Fusiliers	—
Dykes, William	Sergeant	Royal Garrison Artillery ...	—
Espey, Frederick ...	Private	2nd Royal Irish Fusiliers ...	—
Eyres, Albert E. ...	1st Petty Officer, Engine Room Artificer	Royal Naval Reserve	—
Fagan, James	Corporal	East Yorks	—
Farquharson, William ...	Attendant	Royal Naval Sick Berth Reserve	—
Farrell, Patrick ...	Stoker	Royal Naval Reserve	—
***Farrell, Thomas** ...	Gunner	Royal Garrison Artillery ...	—
Farrelly, Patrick ...	Private	Royal Irish Fusiliers	—
Fidler, William	Corporal	Royal Army Medical Corps ...	—

*** Killed in action or died of wounds.**

ENGINEERS' DEPARTMENT *(continued)*.

NAME.	RANK.	REGIMENT.	DECORATION.
Field, William	Driver	Royal Army Service Corps ...	—
Fitzgerald, John ...	Guardsman... ...	2nd Irish Guards	—
Fitzpatrick, John ...	Corporal	Royal Army Service Corps ...	—
Fitzpatrick, Patrick ...	Attendant	Royal Naval Sick Berth Reserve	—
Fitzsimons, John ...	Sergeant	Royal Irish Fusiliers	—
Fitzwilliam, James ...	Able-bodied Seaman	Royal Navy	—
Foley, Michael	Lance-Corporal ...	Royal Army Medical Corps ...	—
Fulham, John	Private	Royal Dublin Fusiliers... ...	—
***Gaster, Henry**	Sergeant-Major ...	10th Essex Regiment	—
Geoghegan, Christopher	Bombardier ...	Royal Field Artillery	—
Geraghty, Thomas ...	Corporal	Royal Army Medical Corps ...	Military Medal.
Graham, William ...	Lance-Corporal ...	Royal Army Medical Corps ...	—
Gray, Robert J.	Sergeant	Royal Air Force...	—
***Griffith, Daniel**	Sergeant	9th Royal Inniskilling Fusiliers	—
Griffith, Francis ...	Private	Royal Irish Fusiliers	—
Grindle, Richard ...	Sick Berth Attendant	Royal Naval Sick Berth Reserve	—
Goodwin, William ...	Sergeant	2nd Essex Regiment	—
Hammond, Charles ...	Private	Royal Army Medical Corps ...	—
Handlon, Thomas ...	Steward	Royal Naval Sick Berth Reserve	—
Hanlon, Peter	Sergeant	2nd Battalion Leinster Regiment	Military Medal. Croix de Guerre.
Hanrahan, Patrick ...	Private	Royal Army Medical Corps ...	—
Hayden, Patrick ...	Steward	Royal Naval Sick Berth Reserve	—
Heaney, Francis ...	Guardsman... ...	Irish Guards	—
Hodgins, James... ...	Private	Royal Irish Fusiliers	—
Hogan, Francis... ...	Private	Royal Army Medical Corps ...	—
Holder, Frederick ...	Private	Middlesex Regiment	—
Holyoake, G. C.... ...	Corporal	Royal Engineers...	Military Medal
Hudson, Gilbert... ...	1st Lieutenant ...	Royal Army Service Corps (M.T.)	—
Hurst, George	Cadet	Officers' Cadet Corps	—
Jameson, Charles W. ...	Private	Royal Air Force...	—
Jordon, Charles... ...	2nd Lieutenant ...	Royal Dublin Fusiliers... ...	—
Jorden, Patrick... ...	Attendant	Royal Naval Sick Berth Reserve	—
Jones, Arthur L. ...	Private	Royal Air Force...	—
Jones, Joseph G. ...	Private	Royal Army Medical Corps ...	—

*** Killed in action or died of wounds.**

ENGINEERS' DEPARTMENT *(continued)*.

NAME.	RANK.	REGIMENT.	DECORATION.
***Kane, Joseph**	Rifleman	Royal Irish Rifles	—
***Kane, Michael**	Corporal	Royal Army Medical Corps ...	—
Kealy, Lawrence ...	Private	Royal Army Medical Corps ...	—
Kearney, Samuel ...	Private	Royal Army Medical Corps ...	—
Kelly, Henry	Leading Telegraph Officer	Royal Navy	—
***Kelly, James**	Private	Royal Dublin Fusiliers... ...	—
Kelly, John	Gunner	Tank Corps	—
Kennedy, Patrick ...	Corporal	Royal Dublin Fusiliers... ...	—
Kiersey, Michael ...	Sergeant	Northumberland Fusiliers ...	Distinguished Conduct Medal.
Kinsella, Thomas ...	Private	Royal Army Medical Corps ...	—
Laffen, John	Sergeant	Royal Dublin Fusiliers... ...	—
***Lamb, Michael J.** ...	Private	7th East Kent Regiment ...	—
Lamb, W. P.	Air Mechanic, 1st Engineer	Royal Naval Air Service ...	—
Law, H. H.	Captain	Royal Dublin Fusiliers... ... Royal Army Service Corps	—
***Lynch, John**	Rifleman	3rd Royal Irish Rifles	—
Macartney, Charles ...	Sergeant	Royal Field Artillery	—
Manders, Andrew ...	Private	Royal Army Medical Corps ...	—
Martin, Charles... ...	Stoker	Royal Navy	—
***Mearns, Patrick** ...	Lance-Corporal ...	Royal Dublin Fusiliers... ...	—
Megahey, Arthur J. ...	Engineer Sub-Lieut.	Royal Naval Reserve	—
Miller, Charles J. ...	Steward	Royal Naval Sick Berth Reserve	—
***Miller, J.**	Captain	6th Royal Welsh Fusiliers ...	—
Mitchell, James... ...	Sergeant	Irish Guards	—
Mockler, Charles ...	Sergeant	Royal Army Medical Corps ...	—
Mockler, Denis ...	Private	Royal Army Medical Corps ...	—
Moore, Thomas ...	Sergeant	South Irish Horse	—
Moran, Patrick	Lance-Corporal ...	Royal Dublin Fusiliers... ...	Distinguished Conduct Medal.
Morrison, Francis ...	Sergeant	Royal Army Medical Corps ...	—
Morton, Francis ...	Steward	Royal Naval Sick Berth Reserve	—
Mulhall, Joseph... ...	Corporal	Royal Munster Fusiliers ...	—
McCaffrey, James ...	Sergeant	Royal Dublin Fusiliers... ...	—
McCormick, Michael ...	Attendant	Royal Naval Sick Berth Reserve	—
***McDonagh, John** ...	Guardsman... ...	1st Irish Guards...	—
***McDonagh, Thomas** ...	Guardsman... ...	1st Irish Guards...	—

*** Killed in action or died of wounds.**

ENGINEERS' DEPARTMENT *(continued)*.

NAME.	RANK.	REGIMENT.	DECORATION.
McGuill, Bernard ...	Sergeant	Royal Dublin Fusiliers... ...	—
McQuade, Michael ...	Q.S....	H.M.S. "Endeavour"... ...	—
Noctor, Michael... ...	1st class Stoker ...	H.M.S. "Galatea"	—
O'Brien John	Steward	Royal Naval Sick Berth Reserve	—
O'Connor, James ...	Private	Royal Army Medical Corps ...	—
O'Connor, James ...	Driver	Royal Field Artillery	—
O'Connor, Thomas J. ...	Ambulance Driver...	Royal Naval Sick Berth Reserve	—
O'Donnell, Pierce ...	Piper	King's Royal Rifles	—
Owens, Bernard ...	Able-bodied Seaman	Royal Naval Reserve	—
Parkinson, William ...	Trooper	11th Hussars	—
Penston, Thomas ...	Rifleman	2nd Royal Irish Rifles	—
Perry, George	Sick Berth Steward	Royal Naval Sick Berth Reserve	—
***Plowman, James** ...	Captain	2nd Leinster Regiment	—
Prestage, James ...	Lance-Corporal ...	Royal Irish Fusiliers	—
***Quinn, John J.**	Gunner	Royal Field Artillery	—
Ray, James	Sergeant	Royal Irish Rifles	—
Reeves, George	Trooper	Royal Irish Lancers	—
Reilly, James E. ...	Sergeant	Irish Guards	—
Reilly, John	Private	Royal Army Medical Corps ...	—
***Reilly, Patrick**	Able-bodied Seaman	Royal Naval Reserve	—
Richardson, Henry ...	Private	Royal Army Medical Corps ...	—
***Riley, John E.**	Private	Royal Army Medical Corps ...	—
Ringwood, Thomas ...	Gunner	Royal Field Artillery	—
Roche, William J. ...	Attendant	Royal Naval Sick Berth Reserve	—
Ronan, Michael... ...	Private	Royal Dublin Fusiliers... ...	—
Sargent, Christopher ...	Sergeant	Royal Dublin Fusiliers... ...	—
Saunders, James ...	Private	Royal Army Medical Corps ...	—
Segrave, H. W.	Captain	Royal Army Service Corps ...	—
***Seiles, John**	Rifleman	1st Royal Irish Rifles	—
Sheehan, John	Trooper	15th Hussars	—
Sheridan, Richard ...	Corporal	Royal Dublin Fusiliers... ...	—
Sheridan, Thomas ...	Private	Royal Dublin Fusiliers... ...	—
Shields, Henry	Engineman	Royal Naval Reserve	—

*** Killed in action or died of wounds.**

ENGINEERS' DEPARTMENT (*continued*).

NAME.	RANK.	REGIMENT.	DECORATION.
Simons, A.	Staff Quarter-Master Sergeant	Royal Army Service Corps ...	—
Slattery, Michael ...	Attendant	Royal Naval Sick Berth Reserve	—
Snedker, George ...	Private	Royal Fusiliers	—
Spillane, Michael ...	Sergeant	Royal Army Medical Corps ...	—
Stevens, Arthur... ...	Rifleman	Rifle Brigade	—
Stevens, F. D.	Major	Royal Air Force...	O.B.E.
Tait, Joseph	Attendant	Royal Naval Sick Berth Reserve Royal Naval Air Service ...	— —
Tait, Robert	Private	Royal Army Medical Corps ...	—
Tapley, Joseph... ...	Steward	Royal Naval Sick Berth Reserve	—
Thomas, Henry... ...	1st class Petty Officer	Royal Naval Sick Berth Reserve	—
Thorpe, John	Private	Royal Army Medical Corps ...	—
Tripp, William E. ...	Company Quarter-Master Sergeant	Royal Fusiliers	—
Tuite, James	Gunner	Royal Field Artillery	—
Turner, T. G.	Captain	Royal Army Service Corps ...	—
Tynan, Michael... ...	Private	Royal Army Medical Corps ...	—
Walker, John	Sergeant	Royal Dublin Fusiliers... ...	—
Wilmot, George... ...	Lance-Corporal ...	Royal Army Medical Corps ...	—
Wilton, George	Regimental Sergeant-Major	South Irish Horse	—
Yarnell, Thomas W. ...	2nd Lieutenant ...	Royal Munster Fusiliers ...	—

FORWARDING DEPARTMENT.

NAME.	RANK.	REGIMENT.	DECORATION.
Anthony, Edward ...	Gunner	Royal Garrison Artillery ...	—
Aylward, William ...	Guardsman... ...	2nd Irish Guards	—
Beasley, Frederick ...	Able-bodied Seaman	Royal Naval Reserve	—
Brandon, Martin ...	Driver	Royal Army Service Corps ...	—
***Broe, Thomas**	Private	1st Royal Dublin Fusiliers ...	—
Brown, Denis	Guardsman... ...	2nd Irish Guards	—
Burke, Edward J. ...	Private	Royal Army Medical Corps ...	Military Medal
Burke, Michael... ...	Private	1st Northumberland Fusiliers...	—
***Byrne, Bernard**... ...	Corporal	Army Cyclist Corps	—
Byrne, Richard... ...	Gunner	Royal Horse Artillery	—
Byrne, Michael... ...	Rifleman	15th Royal Irish Rifles... ...	—

*** Killed in action or died of wounds.**

FORWARDING DEPARTMENT *(continued).*

NAME.	RANK.	REGIMENT.	DECORATION.
Chase, William	Sapper	Royal Engineers...	—
Clampett, James ...	2nd Air Mechanic ...	Royal Air Force...	—
Clarke, Thomas Wm. ...	Cadet	North Staff. Regiment	—
Colgan, Peter	Able-bodied Seaman	Royal Naval Reserve	—
***Connor, Christopher** ...	Leading Seaman ...	Royal Naval Reserve	—
Connor, Thomas H. ...	Sergeant	Royal Field Artillery	—
***Cooke, E. R.**	Captain	8th Royal Irish Fusiliers ...	—
Corcoran, Robert ...	Private	8th South Wales Borderers ...	—
Curran, Christopher ...	Able-bodied Seaman	Royal Fleet Reserve	—
Darcy, Nicholas... ...	Private	1st King's Liverpool	—
Dargan, Bernard ...	Rifleman	1st Royal Irish Rifles	—
***Delaney, Morgan** ...	Guardsman... ...	2nd Irish Guards	—
Domican, George ...	Acting Company Sergeant-Major	2nd Royal Dublin Fusiliers ...	—
Downey, Richard ...	Guardsman... ...	Irish Guards	—
Fitzgerald, John J. ...	Petty Officer ...	Royal Navy	—
Flynn, Peter	Guardsman... ...	2nd Irish Guards	—
Foley, Edward	Corporal	1st Royal Irish Fusiliers ...	—
Geeves, Michael... ...	Company Sergeant-Major	1st Royal Dublin Fusiliers ...	—
Geoghegan, Michael ...	Guardsman... ...	2nd Irish Guards	—
Ginivan, Patrick ...	Private	8th Royal Irish Fusiliers ...	—
Glazier, Robert... ...	Attendant	Royal Naval Volunteer Reserve	—
Gray, Edward	Company Sergeant-Major	3rd Connaught Rangers ...	—
Gray, Robert N. ...	Corporal	6th Royal Dublin Fusiliers ...	—
***Greene, George**... ...	Shoeing Smith ...	Royal Horse Artillery	—
Harte, James	Guardsman... ...	2nd Irish Guards	—
Haslam, William ...	Private	Royal Army Medical Corps ...	—
Haycock, W.	Major	Royal Army Service Corps ...	—
Hilton, Lonie	Warrant Officer ...	Royal Navy	—
Holcroft, Bernard ...	Leading Seaman ...	Royal Navy	—
Keegan, John	Wheeler Corporal...	Royal Army Service Corps ...	—
Kenna, Thomas... ...	Private	Royal Army Medical Corps ...	—
Kenny, Michael... ...	Gunner	Royal Field Artillery	—

*** Killed in action or died of wounds.**

FORWARDING DEPARTMENT *(continued).*

NAME.	RANK.	REGIMENT.	DECORATION.
***Kerins, Patrick**	Private	1st Royal Irish Regiment ...	—
Kiernan, Cecil	Able-bodied Seaman	Royal Naval Reserve	—
Kinsella, James... ...	Guardsman... ...	1st Irish Guards...	—
Knox, John	Guardsman... ...	1st Irish Guards...	—
Lawlor, Patrick ...	Sergeant	2nd Royal Dublin Fusiliers ...	Military Medal.
***Malone, Thomas** ...	Rifleman	2nd Royal Irish Rifles	—
Manning, Joseph ...	Private	8th Royal Dublin Fusiliers ...	—
Mathews, Patrick ...	Shoeing Smith ...	6th Dragoons	—
Murphy, Bernard ...	Guardsman... ...	2nd Irish Guards	—
Murray, Sylvester ...	Wheelwright ...	15th Tank Corps	Military Medal.
McCullagh, Edward ...	Guardsman... ...	Irish Guards	Military Medal.
McCullagh, Laurence ...	Sergeant	1st Royal Irish Fusiliers ...	—
McEvoy, Michael ...	Lance-Corporal ...	2nd Royal Dublin Fusiliers ...	—
Nicholson, Richard ...	Sergeant	Royal Army Medical Corps ...	—
Norton, William... ...	Gunner	Royal Garrison Artillery ...	—
Oates, Richard	Attendant	Royal Naval Sick Berth Reserve	—
***O'Brien, John**	Guardsman... ...	1st Irish Guards...	—
O'Brien, Michael ...	Guardsman... ...	1st Irish Guards...	—
***O'Donnell, Philip** ...	Private	2nd Royal Dublin Fusiliers ...	—
Patrick, Andrew ...	Sergeant	Royal Garrison Artillery ...	Military Medal.
***Pidgeon, George** ...	Private	10th Royal Dublin Fusiliers ...	—
Quinn, Patrick	Lance-Corporal ...	Royal Army Service Corps ...	—
Rea, George	Lance-Corporal ...	9th Royal Irish Fusiliers ...	—
Reynolds, James ...	Able-bodied Seaman	Royal Navy	—
Ryan, James	Guardsman... ...	1st Irish Guards...	—
Scott, A....	Lieutenant	1st Royal Dublin Fusiliers ...	—
Scully, John	Corporal	6th Royal Munster Fusiliers ...	—
***Sheridan, Nicholas** ...	Guardsman... ...	2nd Irish Guards	—
Smith, Michael	Able-bodied Seaman	Royal Fleet Reserve	—
***Stafford, George** ...	Corporal	10th Royal Dublin Fusiliers ...	—
***Stafford, Thomas** ...	Lance-Corporal ...	9th Royal Dublin Fusiliers ...	—

*** Killed in action or died of wounds.**

FORWARDING DEPARTMENT *(continued)*.

NAME.	RANK.	REGIMENT.	DECORATION.
***Taaffe, James**	Private	2nd Royal Munster Fusiliers ...	—
Talbot, Robert	Sergeant	Royal Army Medical Corps ...	—
Tierney, Peter	Corporal	1st Connaught Rangers ...	—
Traynor, Michael ...	Rifleman	8th Royal Irish Rifles	—
Tuite, James	Leading Seaman ...	Royal Naval Reserve	—
Walters, Charles ...	3rd Air Mechanic ...	Royal Air Force...	—
Whelan, David	Gunner	Royal Marine Artillery	—
Whelan, Richard ...	Private	Royal Army Medical Corps ...	—
Williams, Joseph ...	Sergeant	1st Irish Guards	—
Wilson, Frederick ...	Trooper	5th Dragoon Guards	—

HOP FARM.

NAME.	RANK.	REGIMENT.	DECORATION.
Batchup, Arthur H. ...	Private	1st Herts. Regiment	—
Benton, George T. ...	Corporal	7th Royal Engineers	Military Medal.
***Curtis, John P.**	Private	3rd East Kent Regiment ...	—
***Eldridge, Arthur** ...	Guardsman... ...	2nd Coldstream Guards ...	—
***Eldridge, Bertram** ...	Private	16th Royal Sussex Regiment ...	—
Messetter, Samuel ...	Private	36th Royal Fusiliers	—
Munton, John R. ...	Private	Middlesex Regiment	—
Whibley, John	Lance-Corporal ...	13th Royal Sussex Regiment ...	—

MEDICAL DEPARTMENT.

NAME.	RANK.	REGIMENT.	DECORATION.
Coffey, Edward	Staff Sergeant ...	Royal Army Medical Corps ...	—
Delahunty, John ...	2nd Sick Berth Steward	Royal Naval Sick Berth Reserve	—
Ingram, R.	Sick Berth Steward	Royal Naval Sick Berth Reserve	—
Lumsden, Sir John ...	Major	Royal Army Medical Corps ...	K.B.E.
Pepper, G. E.	Captain	Royal Army Medical Corps (S.R.)	Mentioned in Despatches.

*** Killed in action or died of wounds.**

PRINTING DEPARTMENT.

NAME.	RANK.	REGIMENT.	DECORATION.
Brennan, Denis	Senior Attendant ...	Royal Naval Sick Berth Reserve	—
Butler, Reginald ...	Private	Royal Dublin Fusiliers... ...	—
Coughlan, Thomas ...	Senior Attendant ...	Royal Naval Sick Berth Reserve	—
Flower, Walter	Trooper	South Irish Horse	—
***Richardson, Henry** ...	Private	10th Royal Dublin Fusiliers ...	—
Saunders, Thomas A. ...	Corporal	13th Yorks. Regiment	—
Spencer, George ...	Senior Attendant ...	Royal Naval Sick Berth Reserve	—
Waller, James W. ...	Quarter-Master Sergeant	Royal Army Medical Corps ...	Meritorious Service Medal.
Wilkie, David	Lance-Sergeant ...	3rd Royal Irish Fusiliers ...	—

REFRESHMENT DEPARTMENT.

NAME.	RANK.	REGIMENT.	DECORATION.
Burgess, Samuel ...	Sergeant	7th Royal Dublin Fusiliers ...	—
Byrne, Hugh	Guardsman... ...	1st Irish Guards...	—
***Doyle, William**	Gunner	Royal Field Artillery	—
***Dunne, John**	Guardsman... ...	2nd Irish Guards	—
Kelly, Christopher ...	Private	1st East Yorks. Regiment ...	—
Mara, Arthur	Rifleman	2nd Royal Irish Rifles	—
Newham, Maurice ...	Company Sergeant-Major	5th East Kent Regiment ...	Distinguished Conduct Medal.
Robson, Thomas ...	Corporal	Royal Army Medical Corps ...	—

SECRETARY'S DEPARTMENT.

NAME.	RANK.	REGIMENT.	DECORATION.
Carter Percy	Private	Royal Air Force...	—
Corrin, James	Petty Officer ...	Royal Naval Sick Berth Reserve	—
Dempsey, Charles ...	Attendant	Royal Naval Sick Berth Reserve	—
***Drury, W. S.**	Lieutenant	8th Royal Dublin Fusiliers ...	—
Ennis, John M.	Attendant	Royal Naval Sick Berth Reserve	—

*** Killed in action or died of wounds.**

SECRETARY'S DEPARTMENT (*continued*).

NAME.	RANK.	REGIMENT.	DECORATION.
Farrell, Michael ...	Quarter-Master Sergeant	Royal Dublin Fusiliers... ...	—
Graham, Gordon ...	Lance-Corporal ...	Royal Army Service Corps ...	—
Hyland, George	Able-bodied Seaman	Royal Navy	—
Ingram, William R. ...	Private	Royal Air Force...	—
***Jeffreson, V.**	Private	7th Royal Dublin Fusiliers ...	—
Leetch, John	Able-bodied Seaman	Royal Navy	—
Marks, A. K.	Captain	Royal Army Service Corps ...	—
Norman, C. G.	Lieutenant	Royal Dublin Fusiliers... ...	—
Singleton, T.	Lieutenant	Royal Army Service Corps (M.T.)	Mentioned in Despatches.
Wadsworth, H.	Paymaster Lieut. ...	Royal Naval Volunteer Reserve	—

VATHOUSE.

NAME.	RANK.	REGIMENT.	DECORATION.
Ball, Ernest	3rd Air Mechanic ...	Royal Air Force...	—
Coyne, John	Company Sergeant-Major	7th Royal Dublin Fusiliers ...	Meritorious Service Medal.
***Devine, Patrick**... ...	Lance-Corporal ...	1st Northumberland Fusiliers...	—
Farrell, George A. ...	Corporal	Royal Army Medical Corps ...	—
Foley, James	Private	Royal Army Medical Corps ...	—
Garland, E. D.	Captain	Leinster Regiment	—
***Haines, A. C. C.**... ...	2nd Lieutenant ...	2nd Royal Dublin Fusiliers ...	—
Hannon, John	Lance-Corporal ...	4th Queen's Own Hussars ...	Meritorious Service Medal.
Healy, Joseph	Bombardier ...	28th Royal Field Artillery ...	—
***Heaney, Edward** ...	Sergeant	1st Irish Guards...	—
Murray, William ...	Private	9th Royal Dublin Fusiliers ...	—
Reeves, Joseph... ...	1st class Steward ...	Royal Naval Sick Berth Reserve	—
Reilly, Patrick	Private	Royal Army Medical Corps ...	—

*** Killed in action or died of wounds.**

VATHOUSE (*continued*).

NAME.	RANK.	REGIMENT.	DECORATION.
***Sargent, Robert...** ...	Guardsman... ...	1st Irish Guards...	—
Syms, Michael J. ...	Sergeant	Royal Army Medical Corps ...	—
Tutty, Thomas	Private	8th Royal Dublin Fusiliers ...	—
Wallis, George	Private	4th Royal Fusiliers	—
Whelan, John	Sergeant	20th Hussars	—
Woods, R. F.	2nd Lieutenant ...	10th Royal Dublin Fusiliers ... Royal Army Service Corps (M.T.)	—

TRADE STORES.

BELFAST.

NAME.	RANK.	REGIMENT.	DECORATION.
Bennett, William ...	Sergeant	King's African Rifles	—
Follis, John	Guardsman... ...	1st Irish Guards...	—
Hall, Patrick J.... ...	Guardsman... ...	1st Irish Guards...	—
***Hamilton, W.**	Lieutenant	Connaught Rangers	—
***Jameson, William J.** ...	Guardsman... ...	1st Irish Guards...	—
McVicker, James ...	Guardsman... ...	1st Irish Guards...	—
Pinion, E.	2nd Lieutenant ...	15th Royal Irish Rifles... ...	—
Russell, Sidney	Guardsman... ...	1st Irish Guards...	—
***Stritch, Joseph**	Sergeant	Royal Irish Fusiliers	—

BRISTOL.

NAME.	RANK.	REGIMENT.	DECORATION.
Cordner, A. N.	Lieutenant	6th Black Watch (Royal Highlanders)	—
Myles, H. F.	Lieutenant	Royal Army Service Corps ...	—
Sparks, Wm. A. J. ...	Private	Royal Army Medical Corps ...	—
***Wilson, S. R.**	Lieutenant	13th Argyle & Sutherland Highlanders	—

CARDIFF.

NAME.	RANK.	REGIMENT.	DECORATION.
Crotty, Trevor	Captain	Royal Army Service Corps ...	M.B.E.
Sharpe, Archibald J. ...	Private	Royal Army Medical Corps ...	—

*** Killed in action or died of wounds.**

TRADE STORES (*continued*).

NAME.	RANK.	REGIMENT.	DECORATION.
		CORK.	
Barry, E. H.	Captain	Royal Army Service Corps ...	—
***Beatty, B. G.**	2nd Lieutenant ...	Royal Flying Corps	—
***Cross, G. H.**	Captain	Royal Army Service Corps ...	—
Higgins, John	Sergeant	14th Tank Corps	—
		GALWAY.	
Dagg, S. A.	Lance-Corporal ...	Artists' Rifles	—
Lamb, J. G.	Corporal	Despatch Rider, Signal Service, Royal Engineers	—
Mack, Martin	Driver	Royal Army Service Corps ...	—
		GLASGOW.	
Handyside, J. B. ...	Private	3rd Argyle & Sutherland Highlanders	—
McFarlane, Malcolm ...	Private	19th Royal Scots. Fusiliers ...	—
McKeachan, Finlay ...	Gunner	Royal Garrison Artillery ...	—
McNeill, Angus	Able-bodied Seaman	Royal Naval Volunteer Reserve	—
		LIMERICK.	
***Fitzmaurice, A. H.** ...	Lieutenant	1st Reserve Regiment of Lancers (attached Royal Flying Corps)	—
Lawrenson, C. A. ...	Lieutenant	3rd Royal Irish Regiment ...	—
***McCormac, H. H.** ...	Lieutenant	5th Royal Irish Fusiliers ...	—
		LIVERPOOL.	
Adam, R.	2nd Lieutenant ...	Royal Garrison Artillery ...	—
Brown, William H. ...	Private	Royal Welsh Fusiliers	—
Buckley, Denis	Corporal	18th Hussars	—
Cathcart, William ...	Corporal	Royal Army Service Corps ...	—
Connolly, James ...	Private	Royal Army Service Corps ...	—
Deal, William (Cooper)	3rd Air Mechanic ...	Royal Flying Corps	—
Ibbott, John J.	2nd Air Mechanic ...	Royal Air Force...	
Ireland, W. G.	Captain	6th South Lancashire Regiment	—

*** Killed in action or died of wounds.**

TRADE STORES (*continued*).

NAME.	RANK.	REGIMENT.	DECORATION.
		LIVERPOOL *(continued)*.	
Kelly, Joseph	Staff Captain ...	Royal Engineers...	—
***Kelly, Laurence...** ...	Corporal	47th Machine Gun Corps ...	—
Keith, A....	Leadg. Air Mechanic	Royal Naval Air Service ...	—
Major, Robinson ...	Private	Royal Army Service Corps ...	—
Mayne, Thomas... ...	Private	Royal Defence Corps	—
McElhinney, Michael ...	Corporal	Royal Army Service Corps ...	—
McCutcheon, T. A. ...	2nd Lieutenant ...	1st (G) Worcester Regt. ...	—
Rawlins, Henry... ...	Corporal	Royal Welsh Fusiliers	—
Tennant, H. C.	3rd Air Mechanic ...	Royal Air Force...	—
Witz, L. T. P.	Private	23rd Middlesex	—
		LONDON.	
Bennett, W. F.	Lieutenant	9th East Surrey Regiment ...	—
Bolster, L. K.	Lieutenant	Royal Army Service Corps (Horse Transport)	—
Buckley, Thomas E. ...	Corporal	Royal Field Artillery	—
Daly, T. B.	Lieutenant	6th Black Watch (Royal Highlanders)	—
Cooney, F. C.	Lieutenant	Royal Field Artillery (T.) ...	—
Hitchens, R. M.... ...	Captain	8th (Irish) King's Liverpool Regiment (T.F.)	—
Knapton, John J. ...	Sergeant	Royal West Kents	—
Moore, R. L. E.... ...	Captain	Royal Marine Artillery... ...	—
Murray, H. W.	Lieutenant	Royal Naval Volunteer Reserve	Mentioned in Despatches.
Norris, C. P.	Private	17th Essex Regiment	—
Pickering, Ernest F. ...	Staff Sergeant ...	Royal Army Ordnance Corps ...	—
Sharpe, S. P.	Sapper	Royal Engineers...	—
Tichborne, W.	2nd Lieutenant ...	Connaught Rangers	—

*** Killed in action or died of wounds.**

TRADE STORES *(continued)*.

NAME.	RANK.	REGIMENT.	DECORATION.
		LONGFORD.	
***Early, John James** ...	Guardsman	2nd Irish Guards	—
Frazer, D. M.	Captain	3rd Connaught Rangers (Res.)	—
Hanley, Christopher ...	Corporal	Royal Army Service Corps ...	—
Hermanni, G.	Lieutenant	Intelligence Corps	Mentioned in Despatches.
		MANCHESTER.	
Chappell, George H. ...	Private	Royal Air Force...	—
Dunne, E. A.	Bombardier ...	Royal Garrison Artillery ...	—
Major, Arthur	Private	3/7 Manchester Regiment ...	—
McGuinness, Patrick ...	Private	Royal Army Veterinary Corps...	—
O'Loughlin, John ...	Private	25th Manchester Regiment ...	—
Snape, Joseph	Private	Royal Welsh Fusiliers	—
Wilmot, C. G.	Acting-Corporal ...	3rd Cheshire Regiment... ...	—
***Wood, Albert James** ...	Private	1/5th Loyal North Lancs. Regt.	—
		NEWCASTLE-ON-TYNE.	
Dodds, J. S.	Corporal	Royal Army Service Corps ...	—
Herbert, L. A.	Captain	4th Corps Cyclist Battalion Army Cyclist Corps	—
Kennaway, James ...	Corporal	22nd Tank Corps	—
Robertson, Henry ...	Private	13th Yorkshire Regiment ...	—
Stritch, A. J. R. ...	Private	8th Royal Irish Regiment ...	—

*** Killed in action or died of wounds.**

TRADE STORES *(continued)*.

Name.	Rank.	Regiment.	Decoration.
		LONGFORD.	
***Early, John James** ...	Guardsman... ...	2nd Irish Guards	—
Frazer, D. M.	Captain	3rd Connaught Rangers (Res.)	—
Hanley, Christopher ...	Corporal	Royal Army Service Corps ...	—
Hermanni, G.	Lieutenant	Intelligence Corps	Mentioned in Despatches.
		MANCHESTER.	
Chappell, George H. ...	Private	Royal Air Force...	—
Dunne, E. A.	Bombardier ...	Royal Garrison Artillery ...	—
Major, Arthur	Private	3/7 Manchester Regiment ...	—
McGuinness, Patrick ...	Private	Royal Army Veterinary Corps...	—
O'Loughlin, John ...	Private	25th Manchester Regiment ...	—
Snape, Joseph	Private	Royal Welsh Fusiliers	—
Wilmot, C. G.	Acting-Corporal ...	3rd Cheshire Regiment... ...	—
***Wood, Albert James** ...	Private	1/5th Loyal North Lancs. Regt.	—
		NEWCASTLE-ON-TYNE.	
Dodds, J. S.	Corporal	Royal Army Service Corps ...	—
Herbert, L. A.	Captain	4th Corps Cyclist Battalion Army Cyclist Corps	—
Kennaway, James ...	Corporal	22nd Tank Corps	—
Robertson, Henry ...	Private	13th Yorkshire Regiment ...	—
Stritch, A. J. R. ...	Private	8th Royal Irish Regiment ...	—

*** Killed in action or died of wounds.**

APPENDIX I.

On the 16th February, 1920, a deputation of Brewery Workmen waited upon the Chairman of the Company and presented an Illuminated Address, of which the following is a copy:—

TO THE DIRECTORS OF

Messrs. ARTHUR GUINNESS, SON & CO., Ltd.

DUBLIN.

FEBRUARY, 1920.

We, the employees of Messrs. A. Guinness, Son & Company, Limited, who left their employment to serve in His Majesty's Forces in the late European War, hereby tender our sincere thanks to the Directors and Board of the Firm for their unfailing generosity and kindness to us, our wives and families, during our absence on Service, and for their patriotic action in keeping open and reinstating their employees in the positions they occupied previous to the War.

We assure the Directors and Board of our grateful loyalty and devotion to the interests of the Company.

BREWHOUSE DEPARTMENT.

Armstrong,	Edward.
Byrne,	Patrick.
Brien,	William.
Brien,	Michael.
Brien,	James.
Callan,	William.
Collins,	Edward.
Comerford,	Patrick.
Conway,	Charles.
Curran,	John.
Delaney,	Richard.
Dunne,	Michael.
Darlington,	William.
Farrell,	Joseph.
Harrington,	Patrick.

BREWHOUSE DEPT., continued.

King,		Timothy.
Kinnear,		William.
Keeley,		James.
Lott,		Thomas.
Martin,		Peter.
Murray,		John.
McManus,		Thomas.
McSherry,		Michael.
O'Connor,		John.
Redmond,		Stephen.
Ryan,		Andrew.
Stephens,		Robert.
Switzer,	M.C., M.S.M.,	Robert.
Stafford,		George.
Scally,		Edward.
Woods,	D.S.M.,	George.

ENGINEERS' DEPARTMENT.

Bonny,		John.
Brennan,		Denis.
Duffy,		James.
Devitt,		John.
Downes,		James.
Durkin,		Thomas.
Doyle,		John.
Dennison,		Patrick.
Domican,	M.M.,	John.
Fitzpatrick,		John.
Fitzsimons,		John.
Farquharson,		William.
Foley,		Michael.
Graham,		William.
Grindle,		Richard.
Geraghty,	M.M.,	Thomas.
Handlon,		Thomas.
Hanrahan,		Patrick.
Heaney.		Francis.
Kennedy,		Patrick.
Macartney,		Charles.
Martin,		Charles.
Morton,		Francis.
Moran,	D.C.M.,	Patrick.
Mulhall,		Joseph.
McQuade,		Michael.
McCaffrey,		James.
McCormick,		Michael.
Noctor,		Michael.
O'Brien,		John.
Reeves,		George.
Richardson,		Henry.
Shields,		Henry.
Stevens,		Arthur.
Sheridan,		Richard.
Saunders,		James.
Tait,		Joseph.
Tait,		Robert.
Thorpe,		John.
Tuite,		James.
Walker,		John.

ENGINEERS' TRADES DEPARTMENT.

Eyres,	Albert.
Bluett,	Sidney.
Bray,	Digby.
Cashell,	Robert.
Cooney,	Thomas.

ENGINEERS' TRADES DEPT., continued.

Coole,	William J.
Corrin,	Henry.
Dykes,	William.
Gray,	Robert J.
Graham,	William.
Hogan,	Francis.
Jordan,	Charles.
Kearney,	Samuel.
Mockler,	Denis.
Thompson,	Thomas.
Tynan,	Michael.

COOPERAGE DEPARTMENT.

Byrne,	William.
Byrne,	Henry.
Byrne,	Denis.
Byrne,	Bernard.
Byrne,	Myles.
Brown,	Samuel.
Clarke,	Christopher.
Connolly,	Thomas.
Connolly,	Thomas.
Culverhouse,	Francis.
Cunningham,	Thomas.
Cunningham,	Henry.
Daly,	Thomas.
Doyle,	John.
Doyle,	Patrick.
Gogarty,	Francis.
Hammond,	Charles.
Fox,	Patrick.
Helly,	John.
Halford,	Francis.
Hanlon,	Peter.
Keeble,	Albert.
King,	Charles.
Kavanagh,	Thomas.
Kelly,	Michael.
Lacey,	Edward.
Morgan,	Joseph.
Murray,	Robert.
Moore,	Thomas.
McGuire,	John.
McDonald,	William.
Ormonde,	Philip.
Price,	Patrick.
Stynes,	Joseph.
Traynor,	George.
Woodhead,	Charles.

COOPERS' DEPARTMENT.

Carroll,		Michael.
Carroll,		Michael J.
Campbell,		James.
Cleary,		Thomas.
Coffey,		James.
Cosgrove,		James.
Curran,		Nicholas.
Delaney,		Edward.
Dunn,		Patrick.
Dunne,		Stephen.
Hegarty,		Joseph.
Hendrick,		Patrick.
Hill,	D.C.M., M.M.,	Joseph.
Hogan,		Michael.
Joyce,		Augustine.
Lynch,	M.M.,	Thomas.
McFarlane,		William.
O'Dea,		Michael.
O'Connor,		John P.
O'Connor,		James.
Pinkerton,		David.
Powell,		Joseph.
Powell,		James.
Russell,		Dominick.
Simpson,		Michael.
Stokes,	C. de G.,	John.
Tait,	D.C.M., M.M.,	Thomas.
Quinn,		Bernard J.

FORWARDING DEPARTMENT.

Aylward,		William.
Anthony,		Edward.
Brandon,		Martin.
Byrne,		Richard.
Brown,		Denis.
Corcoran,		Robert.
Coyne,	M.M.,	Francis.
Domican,		George.
Dargan,		Bernard.
Gray,		Edward.
Geeves,		Michael.
Haslam,		William.
Holcroft,		Bernard.
Kenny,		Michael.
Kenna,		Thomas.
Lawlor,	M.M.,	Patrick.
Murray,	M.M.,	Sylvester.
Murphy,		Bernard.
McEvoy,		Michael.
McCullagh,		Laurence.
McCullagh,	M.M.,	Edward.

FORWARDING DEPT., continued.

Noctor,		M.
Oates,		Richard.
Patrick,	M.M.,	Andrew.
Quinn,		Patrick.
Scully,		John.
Tierney,		Peter.
Williams,		Richard.

VATHOUSE, VICTORIA QUAY.

Coyne,	M.S.M.,	John.
Farrell,		George.
Foley,		James.
Hannon,	M.S.M.,	John.
Healy,		Joseph.
Murray,		William.
Reeves,		Joseph.
Reilly,		Patrick.
Wallis,		George.
Whelan,		John.

COOKE'S LANE MALTINGS.

Byrne,		John
Doonan,		William.
Hennessey,		Thomas.
Nolan,		John.
Powderly,		Christopher.

PRINTING DEPARTMENT.

Butler,		Reginald.
Coughlan,		Thomas.
Spencer,		George.
Waller,	M.S.M.,	James W.
Wilkie,		David.

OFFICES DEPARTMENT.

Corrin,		James.
Dempsey,		Charles.
Graham,		Gordon.
Buckley,		Francis.

CASK DEPARTMENT.

Walker,		Henry.

MEDICAL DEPARTMENT.

Coffey,	**Edward.**
Delahunty,	**John.**

TRADE STORES.

Follis,	**John.**	*Belfast.*
Hall,	**Patrick.**	,,
McVicker,	**James.**	,,
Higgins,	**John.**	*Cork.*
Hanley,	**Christopher.**	*Longford.*
Sharpe,	**Archibald.**	*Cardiff.*
McNeill,	**Angus.**	*Glasgow.*
McKeachan,	**Finlay.**	,,
McFarlane,	**Malcolm.**	,,
Brown,	**William.**	*Liverpool.*
Deal, (Cooper)	**William.**	,,

TRADE STORES, continued.

Ibbott,	**John J.**	*Liverpool.*
Kelly,	**Joseph.**	,,
Major,	**Robinson.**	,,
Rawlins,	**Henry.**	,,
Mayne,	**Thomas.**	,,
Buckley,	**Thomas E.**	*London.*
Knapton,	**John F.**	,,
Pickering.	**Ernest F.**	,,
Chappell,	**George H.**	*Manchester.*
McGuinness,	**Patrick.**	,,
O'Loughlin,	**John.**	,,
Snape,	**Joseph.**	,,
Kennaway,	**James.**	*Newcastle-on-Tyne.*
Robertson,	**Henry.**	,,

HOP FARM.

Batchup,		**Arthur H.**
Benton,	**M.M.,**	**George.**
Messetter,		**Samuel.**
Munton,		**John R.**

A number of employees who had not an opportunity of subscribing to the address in the first instance desired to express their thanks in a similar manner, and accordingly a duplicate address was prepared, and the two hang side by side in the Board Room at James's Gate, Dublin. The names on the supplementary address are as follows:—

BREWHOUSE DEPARTMENT.

Browner,	Thomas.
Burns,	Martin.
Donnelly,	Joseph.
Doyle,	Joseph.
Geraghty,	Thomas.
Gully,	John.
Hogan,	Michael.
Hughes,	Anthony.
Kelly,	William.
Kilfoyle,	William.
McDonnell,	John.
Murphy,	John.
Robinet,	Charles.
Shirley,	Henry.
Smith,	John.
Turnbull,	James.
Wilson,	George.

ENGINEERS' DEPARTMENT.

Breen,	James.
Burke,	William.
Byrne,	Patrick J.
Byrne,	James.
Carroll, D.C.M., M.M.,	William.
Christian,	Patrick.
Coleman,	Patrick.
Costello,	Joseph.
Costello,	Martin.
Cronin,	John.
Cullen,	Thomas.
Daly,	James.
Daly,	Daniel J.
Delaney,	Thomas.
Doherty,	Patrick.
Doyle,	Christopher.

ENGINEERS' DEPT., continued.

Doyle,	Richard.
Duffy,	Luke.
Duke,	John.
Dunne,	Peter.
Dunne,	Thomas E.
Espey,	Frederick.
Farrell,	Patrick.
Farrelly,	Patrick.
Fagan,	James.
Fidler,	William.
Field,	William.
Fitzpatrick,	Patrick.
Fitzwilliam,	James.
Flower,	Walter.
Geoghegan,	Christopher.
Griffith,	Francis.
Hanlon, M.M., C. de G.,	Peter.
Hayden,	Patrick.
Holder,	Frederick.
Jameson,	Charles W.
Jones,	Arthur L.
Jones,	Joseph G.
Jordan,	Patrick.
Kealy,	Laurence.
Kelly,	Henry.
Kiersey,	Michael.
Laffan,	John.
McGuill,	Bernard.
Manders,	Andrew.
Miller,	Charles J.
Mitchell,	James.
Mockler,	Charles.
O'Connor,	Thomas J.
O'Connor,	James.
O'Connor,	James.
O'Donnell,	Pierce.

ENGINEERS' DEPT., continued.

Perry,		George.
Ray,		James.
Roche,		William J.
Ronan,		Michael.
Reilly,		John.
Ringwood,		Thomas.
Sargent,		Christopher.
Sheehan,		John.
Sheridan,		Thomas.
Snedker,		George.
Spillane,		Michael.
Tapley,		Joseph.
Thomas,		Henry.
Tripp,		William E.
Wilmot,		George.

COOPERAGE DEPARTMENT.

Brady,		William.
Brown,		Edward.
Carr,		Joseph.
Farrelly,		Patrick.
Hogan,		Joseph.
Redmond,		William.

FORWARDING DEPARTMENT.

Buckley,		Denis.
Burke,		Michael.
Burke,	M.M.,	Edward J.
Byrne,		Michael.
Chase,		William.
Clampett,		James.
Colgan,		Peter.
Curran,		Christopher.
Darcy,		Nicholas.
Downey,		Richard.
Edwards,		Richard.
Fitzgerald,		John J.
Foley,		Edward.

FORWARDING DEPT., continued.

Glazier,		Robert.
Gray,		Robert N.
Harte,		James.
Hilton,		Lonie.
Keegan,		John P.
Kiernan,		Cecil.
Kinsella,		James.
Knox,		John.
Manning,		Joseph.
Mathews,		Patrick.
Nicholson,		Richard F.
Norton,		William.
O'Brien,		Michael.
Rea,		George.
Reynolds,		James.
Ryan,		James.
Smith,		Michael.
Traynor,		Michael.
Tuite,		James.
Walters,		Charles.
Whelan,		David.
Whelan,		Richard.
Wilson,		Frederick.

VATHOUSE, VICTORIA QUAY.

Ball,		Ernest.
Syms,		Michael J.

PRINTING DEPARTMENT.

Kenny,		John.
Saunders,		Thomas A.

REFRESHMENT DEPARTMENT.

Byrne,		Hugh.
Kelly,		Christopher.
Mara,		Arthur.
Newman,	D.C.M.,	Maurice.

The Earl of Iveagh, K.P., on the occasion of the presentation of the foregoing, replied to the deputation as follows :—

My Friends,

I am anxious, in the first place, to express the pleasure it affords me to meet you here to-day, recognising, as I do, the friendly spirit which has induced you and those who have been working with you to prepare and submit the kind and flattering address which you have just presented. It will always be valued as showing the friendly feelings existing between the Board and those of our Employees who volunteered to go and fight for those of us at home, in the Great War.

Need I say how glad we are to have this opportunity of personally telling you how much we appreciated your patriotic spirit in voluntarily going out to face the dangers and hardships you went through, and how much we rejoice to see you back with us safe and well.

I am proud to think that in all my long life there have been no misunderstandings or troubles as between us and those who have worked for us and so loyally with us in the past. I earnestly trust that in the future those happy relations will always be continued.

I again thank you heartily on my own behalf and on behalf of the other members of the Board.

APPENDIX II.

Staff and Employees killed or died while on Military or Naval Service.

ACCOUNTANT'S DEPARTMENT.

Birmingham, W. A.	6th Royal Irish Fusiliers.
Ward, B. L.	2nd Royal Dublin Fusiliers.

BREWHOUSE DEPARTMENT.

Bligh, Thomas	2nd Battalion Coldstream Guards.
Boland, John	2nd Irish Guards.
Burke, John	2nd Dragoon Guards.
Byrne, Laurence	R.A.M.C.
Conville, Patrick	R.G.A.
Johnston, Robert...	5th Lancers.
Kavanagh, James	1st Irish Guards.
Leslie, Robert	11th Inniskilling Fusiliers.
Mahon, Matt.	2nd Irish Guards.
Noble, John	1st Irish Guards.
Reddy, Francis	1st Yorks and Lancs Regiment.
Ryan, Wm....	1st Irish Guards.
Sinclair, Alex	6th Connaught Rangers.
Stafford, Francis	6th Royal Irish Rifles.
Sheil, C.	Royal Air Force.

CASK DEPARTMENT.

Howard, George	10th Royal Dublin Fusiliers.
Yarnell, V. F. H....	South Irish Horse.

COOKE'S LANE MALTINGS.

Holt, John H.	2/6th North Stafford Regiment.
Kennedy, James	1st Royal Dublin Fusiliers.

COOPERAGE DEPARTMENT.

Brien, Patrick	6th Royal Dublin Fusiliers.
Carlson, Wilson V.	Tank Corps.
Foran, Thos. J.	R.A.M.C.

COOPERAGE DEPARTMENT, continued.

Foster, John ... ... 1st Royal Irish Rifles.
Heffernan, Martin ... ... 9th Royal Dublin Fusiliers.
Hoare, Joseph ... ... 1st Irish Guards.
Hopkins, James ... ... 8th Royal Dublin Fusiliers.
Kerr, William ... ... R.A.M.C.
Leahy, John ... ... 1st Irish Guards.
Mulligan, Alex ... ... 2nd Royal Inniskilling Fusiliers.
Murphy, Thos. ... ... R.F.A.
McIvor, James ... ... 12th King's Royal Rifles.
Nelson, Wm. R. ... ... R.E.
Niland, Joseph ... ... R.E.
O'Rourke, Peter ... ... 2nd Irish Guards.
O'Toole, James ... ... 8th Royal Dublin Fusiliers.
Ryan, Patrick ... ... 2nd Irish Guards.
Sheehan, William ... ... 1st Battalion Rifle Brigade.
Waters, Alex ... ... R.E.
Whelan, Patrick ... ... 2nd Royal Dublin Fusiliers.
White, John ... ... 2nd Royal Irish Regiment.

ENGINEER'S DEPARTMENT.

Boland, Patrick ... ... 1st Royal Irish Rifles.
Devoy, Michael ... ... 9th King's Royal Rifle Corps.
Domican, Richard ... . R.A M.C.
Doyle, Michael C. ... ... R.N.S.B.R.
Farrell, Thomas ... ... R.G.A.
Gaster, Henry ... ... 10th Essex Regiment.
Griffith, Daniel .. .. 9th Royal Inniskilling Fusiliers.
Kane, Joseph ... ... Royal Irish Rifles.
Kane, Michael ... ... R.A.M.C.
Kelly, James ... ... 7th Royal Dublin Fusiliers.
Lamb, Ml. J. ... . 7th East Kent Regiment.
Lynch, John .. .. 3rd Royal Irish Rifles.
Mearns, Patrick ... ... Royal Dublin Fusiliers.
Miller, J. ... ... 6th Royal Welsh Fusiliers.
McDonagh, John ... ... 1st Irish Guards.
McDonagh, Thomas ... ... 1st Irish Guards.
Plowman, James ... ... 2nd Leinster Regiment.
Quinn, John J. ... ... R.F.A.
Reilly, Patrick ... ... R.N.R.
Riley, John E. ... ... R.A.M.C.
Seiles, John .. .. 1st Royal Irish Rifles.

FORWARDING DEPARTMENT.

Broe, Thomas	1st Royal Dublin Fusiliers.
Byrne, Bernard	Army Cyclist Corps.
Connor, Chris.	R.N.R.
Cooke, E. R.	8th Royal Irish Fusiliers.
Davey, Fred W.	R.N.R.
Delaney, Morgan	2nd Irish Guards.
Greene, George	R.H.A.
Kendall, Ernest A.	Royal Naval Reserve.
Kerins, Patrick	1st Royal Irish Regiment.
Malone, Thomas	2nd Royal Irish Rifles.
O'Brien, John	1st Irish Guards.
O'Donnell, Philip	2nd Royal Dublin Fusiliers
Pidgeon, George	10th Royal Dublin Fusiliers.
Sheridan, Nicholas	2nd Irish Guards.
Stafford, George	10th Royal Dublin Fusiliers.
Stafford, Thomas	9th Royal Dublin Fusiliers.
Taaffe, James	2nd Royal Munster Fusiliers.

HOP FARM.

Curtis, John P.	3rd East Kent Regiment.
Eldridge, Arthur	2nd Coldstream Guards.
Eldridge, Bertram	16th Royal Sussex Regiment.

PRINTING DEPARTMENT.

Richardson, Henry	10th Royal Dublin Fusiliers.

REFRESHMENT DEPARTMENT.

Doyle, William	R.F.A.
Dunne, John	2nd Irish Guards.

SECRETARY'S DEPARTMENT.

Drury, W. S.	8th Royal Dublin Fusiliers.
Jeffreson, V.	7th Royal Dublin Fusiliers.

VATHOUSE, VICTORIA QUAY.

Devine, Patrick	1st Northumberland Fusiliers.
Haines, A. C. C.	2nd Royal Dublin Fusiliers.
Heaney, Edward	1st Irish Guards.
Sargent, Robert	1st Irish Guards.

TRADE STORES.

Belfast.

Hamilton, W. ... ... Connaught Rangers.
Jameson, Wm. J. ... ... 1st Irish Guards.
Stritch, Jos. ... ... Royal Irish Fusiliers.

Bristol.

Wilson, S. R. ... ... 13th Argyle and Sutherland Highlanders.

Cork.

Beatty, B. G. ... . R.F.C.
Cross, G. H. ... ... R.A.S.C.

Limerick.

Fitzmaurice, A. H. ... ... 1st Res. Regt. of Lancers attd. R.F.C.
McCormac, H. H. ... . 5th Royal Irish Fusiliers.

Liverpool.

Kelly, Laurence ... . 47th Machine Gun Corps.

Longford.

Early, John James ... ... 2nd Irish Guards.

Manchester.

Wood, Albert James ... ... 1/5th Loyal North Lancashire Regiment.

www.ingramcontent.com/pod-product-compliance
Ingram Content Group UK Ltd.
Pitfield, Milton Keynes, MK11 3LW, UK
UKHW051129260726
13967UKWH00010B/2945